hb.

Bishops Hull,
16th Aug. '11.

79   Flatners. — 82 Woodspring Bay.

137.   Thatching.

17   - George & willows.

43   Spiling the river bank, and 41.

114   coracle in reed bed. 108 up to one's waist ---

72   Stolford fisherman. 76

56   Cricket bat willows

166   Prize conservationists.

187-8 Work at Henn Wall N.R. in 2002

200 Carymoor - for teaching - school visits.

Withy, Rush & Reed
A SOMERSET LEVELS LEGACY

Caroline Bagias

HALSGROVE

First published in Great Britain in 2003

Title page photograph: *Winter flood at North Moor, Othery, 1996*

British Library Cataloguing-in-Publication Data
A CIP record for this title is available from the British Library

ISBN 1 84114 289 1

HALSGROVE

Halsgrove House
Lower Moor Way
Tiverton, Devon EX16 6SS
Tel: 01884 243242
Fax: 01884 243325
email: sales@halsgrove.com
website: www.halsgrove.com

Printed by D'Auria Industrie Grafiche Spa, Italy

Foreword

Our passion for describing and celebrating the places we know and the people we meet has been the inspiration for countless creative acts – in literature, music, painting and, not least, photography. Rural England has been especially powerful as a source of ideas and images. Caroline Bagias' work on the Somerset Levels reminds one immediately of the Victorian photographer Dr Peter Henry Emerson. Emerson depicted with insight and sympathy the life of similar Fenland people, setting and taking up their fishing nets, shooting duck and snipe, gathering reeds and hay, ploughing and harvesting. He believed in 'naturalism', the value of truth to Nature, in contrast to the excessive manipulations of many fine-art photographers of his times, and his finest book *Life and Landscape of the Norfolk Broads* was published in 1886.

Another eminent Victorian, John Ruskin, dismissed photography as a mere mechanical act and managed to have photographers excluded from the group of creative artists who were to benefit from the first Copyright Act, when it was framed in the mid-nineteenth century. Fortunately the creative value of photography is now recognised worldwide.

Taking photographs is only partly a mechanical act. When the photographer is out in the field, on the moor or inside a workshop, the making of an image is a sensitive and complex task. He or she has to work with many potentially conflicting factors and to select moments relating to the direction and intensity of light, movement or position, mood, and the rapid and subtly changing moments of interaction with other people. Whether the photographer sets out to manipulate or control, or to intuitively select, the choices made create a fiction. This is even more the case when the medium is monochrome, a form of abstraction from colourful reality.

Caroline has edited the negatives and prints for this book, manipulated them into sequences and finally given the whole further depth of meaning by adding captions and text. *Withy, Rush and Reed* emerges as a complex narrative about special people with skills that most of us can only marvel at, whose lives are based upon economies that are difficult to sustain, but who create objects, or take part in acts, of considerable beauty.

I hope that this volume will support and encourage all those who can play a part in the survival and future flourishing of the lives of the people and skills so vividly illustrated here.

BARRY LANE
Former Secretary General of the
Royal Photographic Society
March 2003

Dedication

This book is dedicated to those who have kept tradition alive and to those who actively support and value community and rural heritage.

Ted Pitman, coracle maker, 2002

Contents

Acknowledgements

I am indebted to the following for their invaluable help: Ted Pitman, Tim Morgan, George David, James and Nigel Hector, Ken Pimm, Ray Winchester, Ben Coles, Darren Cooke, Les, Mike, Ellen, Jack and Holly Musgrove, John Dye, Brian Lock, Roderick Hector, George Wright, Rob Chambers, Nick Taylor, Peter Woodberry, Tim Edmunds, Domenico Carrone, Andrew Hill, Karen Moule, Darrell Hill, Aubrey Hill, Adrian and Cane Sellick, Brendan Sellick, Bruce Scott, Tony James, John Nash, Ian Mayes, Mrs Cattle, Serena de la Hey, Lucy Watten, Guy Martin, Ian Strugnell, Kate Lynch, Peter Nicholas, John Trenchard, Beryl Eaton, David Eaton, Andy Carter, Belinda, Hannah, Matthew and Mark Humphry, Lorraine Houlden, Geoff Rice, Jennifer John, Caroline Brown, Hilary Burns, Jo Hynes, Christopher Amey, Sook Shackleton, Jill Wilkinson, Linda Lemieux, Philip Geers, Sarah Pank, Graham Wilkinson, Lyn Edwards, John Excell, Harold, Richard, Dennis, Andrew and David Wright, Tom Rymer, George Willis, Dave Franklin, Martin Dunster, Keith Payne, Ben Hammett, Royston Binding, Paul Biddiscombe, Daniel Bishop, Richard Fryer, Nigel and Mac Day, Gerry and David Masters, Ben Malin, Graham Mitchell, Melvin Yeandle, Richard Bradford, Jonathan Coate, Marcus Frankpitt, Sally Mills, Mike Johnson, Henry and Richard Lang, Jill Gilbert, Hamish Craig, Barbara Jones, Bill Poirrier, Tristan Elki, Ed Hooper, Barry Lane, Sue Isherwood, John Letts and my good friends Neville Whitney, Kay Berry and Jean Tungate.

Special thanks go to The Levels and Moors Partnership (LAMP) for financing the photographic materials and South West Arts for their contribution towards research and development.

The author would also like to acknowledge the following titles which have proved useful in the compilation of this volume: Christopher Newsholme's *The Genus Salix*, Douglas A. Watling's *The Life and Times of the Cricket Bat Willow*, Johnson, Barratt and Butcher's *Chair Seating, Norfolk Reed*, produced by the Master Thatchers Association, and Judy Nash's *Thatchers and Thatching*.

Tim Morgan, Athelney Farm, 2001; after grading, teasles were tied in handfuls in the shape of a half-moon and attached to long poles before being secured with a band of withy.

Introduction

Back in 1998, when I first began to photograph the rush cutting on the River Isle, I never imagined that five years later the project would lead to the publication of a book such as this. My interest in social documentary photography must have begun then, for I have continued ever since to find subjects that I felt needed to be photographed.

As my photography has progressed I have increasingly come to realise how important it is to record the simple, everyday events as well as the special occasions. Those familiar with the work of James Ravilious, who sadly died in 1999, will understand what I mean. He has, along with Frank Meadow-Sutcliff and Emerson, recorded every imaginable aspect of life within his particular community. Traditional monochrome photography is surely the best medium for this kind of work, which is, fortunately, now enjoying more widespread recognition. Such photography is, alongside some of the skills documented in this book, a craft in itself which requires greater recognition. The modern history of mankind has, to a great extent, been documented in photographs, mostly by means of the monochrome process. This too could be in danger of being lost with the advent of modern technologies.

Many of the individuals portrayed in this book belong to a diminishing group in possession of a rare knowledge of nature and rural skills which have been handed down from generation to generation; a heritage which if not passed on may be lost. In some instances the younger generations continue to follow in their fathers' footsteps. However, many of them will probably find more lucrative ways of earning a living. I was heartened to discover how many young people are actively involved one way or another in these traditional practices. The roots of our local economy undoubtedly lie in the land and with those who clearly still hold many of its secrets. I hope that this body of work will go towards demonstrating how these skills remain very much a part of our rural economy today and that they are not simply regarded as nostalgic relics of the past.

My inspiration is Julia Margaret Cameron; I keep reminding myself that she was 48 years old when she took up photography and in only a decade or so produced some of the finest photographic work that exists today. It is my wish to give a voice to people who cannot speak for themselves or whose voices cannot be heard, and, much as I hope that my pictures will be used to inform future generations, I also want them to be enjoyed.

CAROLINE BAGIAS
AUGUST 2003

Willow track to Stoke St Gregory, 1998

Withy: 2000–02

The Somerset Levels and Moors are rich in history, tradition and character. Today's landscape has been shaped by human efforts to reclaim the land for agriculture, especially since the Middle Ages. Ditches or rhynes act as 'wet fences' in the summer and drainage channels for flooding in the winter. Throughout the ages, both people and wildlife have adapted to this wet environment, which often results in flooding and villages being cut off for weeks at a time.

Ever since the sea retreated more than 6,000 years ago, willow (*salix*), which has a three-year rotation period as opposed to hazel which requires seven years to mature, has been grown on the Somerset Levels, and the willow-weaving skills, which date back to the Bronze Age, are still in use at the start of the twenty-first century. Willows planted alongside roads and droves have come to be used as landmarks in times of flood. Pollarding (the annual harvesting of shoots) provides willow for thatching spars, hurdles and firewood.

Salix thrive mostly in moist habitats. However, they tolerate long periods of drought and will even grow on infertile, compacted and poorly drained land. They are great survivors with enormous powers of regeneration, their spreading roots acting effectively during flooding. They are often used to revitalise desolate areas such as those left by open-cast mining and disused gravel pits.

Propagation

Withies are grown as shrubs rather than trees. In March and April one-year-old rods (sets), 18ins in length, are planted leaving a third of their length above soil level and measurements between rows are calculated to allow space for mechanical cultivators. Harvesting has traditionally been done by hand and a few willow growers continue this practice today. However, the larger firms harvest the coppiced withies by machine and grow taller varieties.

For the first two years, shoots are cut back during the winter to encourage new growth. The first rods harvested for commercial use are cut during the winter of the third season when they are pruned to ground level between November and early April to grow the following season.

Ecology

Willow has historically enjoyed many uses and still plays a very versatile and necessary role in the twenty-first century. Crafts associated with the willow industry can be traced back in Great Britain to the Celts; willow has been used to make hurdles, crab and lobster pots, eel traps, coracles and baskets, some of which played an important role during the Second World War. More notable willow products dating from recent times include hot-air balloon baskets and cricket bats. In a number of European countries willow wood has replaced oil as a fuel for industrial and domestic use, and the ancient skill of coppicing is widely encouraged. The British Government's Rural White Paper advocates that 25,000 hectares of short-rotation willow, poplar coppice or *miscanthus* (an energy grass from South East Asia) be planted as part of an Energy Crop Scheme.

Willow is a provider of nectar and pollen for bees early in the year, and old unpruned, polled tree trunks provide nesting sites, whilst an accumulation of organic matter assists the growth of fungi, lichens and ferns. Throughout their lives the willows support a vast ecological cycle of creatures. The traditional uses of willow have been diversified; now they provide garden features and have recently been used along river banks in Somerset and throughout the United Kingdom to help prevent erosion and encourage new vegetation and wildlife. Willow continues to have an important place in the Somerset landscape today, much as it did in times past; it has adapted to change in order to survive.

Basketry

During the Napoleonic Wars the English willow industry came to the fore, with production peaking around the 1960s. Disastrous floods in

1953 and the importation of foreign wares contributed to the decline of the local willow industry. The main willow-growing area today is on the Somerset Levels.

Varieties used for basketry include: the almond-leaved willow, which yields rods 7ft in length, the purple osier, which is tough with thin small rods approximately 3ft long and which is used for fine work, and the common osier which has thick 12ft rods, used mainly for hurdles and agricultural baskets. Rods from the female plant are faster growing and stronger than those from the male plant.

Depending on the colour required and final use, rods may be boiled, untouched, or soaked and stripped of their bark to give browns, buffs and white. Stripping is carried out by mechanical means on a willow brake. The stripped rods are then dried, sorted and tied ready for distribution.

Willow Charcoal

Another highly commercial willow product is artists' charcoal for drawing. This is made by the well-known family firm, Coates, who can be found on the Somerset Levels.

George David and Gordon Butt, Sunny Farm, 2000

George David cutting willow at Aller Moor near Burrowbridge, 2000

Cutting the willow by hand

George David preparing a tie

Harvesting willow

Loading willow

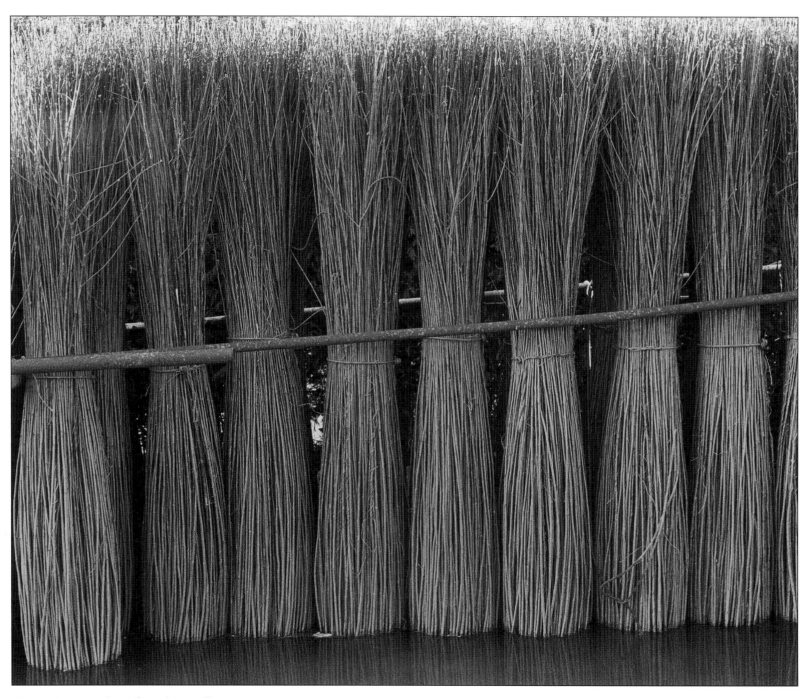

'Pitting' or 'ponding' for white willow

George David, Sunny Farm, Burrowbridge, 2000

George David's withy boiler

Withies are boiled in long tanks for several hours

Sorting willow (grading it for length)

Boiling willow, which is stained buff or brown by the tannin in the bark

George David climbs a ladder to reach the open-topped tank

Removing boiled willow for stripping

This belt drives the 'willow brake' (stripping machine)

Stripping willow

Hands of time

Sorting stripped willow

Carrying stripped willow

A hedge is used (as in days gone by) to support and dry stripped willow

Tying stripped and dried willow by hand

Carrying the tied, stripped and dried willow from the darkened storage shed

George David shares peppermints with Charlie

A specimen hurdle made by English Hurdle

English Hurdle and Willowbank

Erosion and Conservation Services

Father-and-son team Nigel and James Hector run English Hurdle, which was started up by Nigel's father Cecil. He bought an ancient farmhouse with 100 acres of land on the Somerset Levels and became a major supplier of willow for baskets. At the time of writing Nigel lives in the property and the farm buildings and land are used by the company. James Hector says:

Today we have successfully revived traditional hurdle making and provide woven willow garden products. We employ 20 people, half of whom weave hurdles. Our willow beds are clustered over the moors and the willow plants can produce stems for up to 30 years if they are cut back to ground level annually. Harvesting the willow by hand used to be a back-breaking job. This has to a large degree been replaced by machinery.

As part of our ongoing quest to improve the performance of our products we are now using two different varieties of willow in our hurdle production. Willow hurdles can be used to make an attractive screen or fence or to disguise an ugly, albeit utilitarian part of the garden.

One of our favourite sights and scents of summer comes in the form of old-fashioned sweet peas twisting up one of our willow conicals. We have ours planted in attractive pots either side of the kitchen door. We also innovate, not just in garden products but also with our erosion control company, Willowbank.

Willowbank is a five-year-old spin-off business whose staff have established a strong reputation for their skills and know-how in adapting an age-old technique known as 'spiling'. Spiling provides public and private landowners with a speedy, relatively inexpensive installation; a more environmentally acceptable solution to erosion problems.

The Hectors' success story comes at a time when much of Britain's land-based industry seems to be in a state of decline. By using a traditional craft and a renewable resource they are able to provide a service that meets modern demands. It is obvious that willow has as deserved a place in the landscape today as it did thousands of years ago.

James and Nigel Hector, Curload, Stoke St Gregory, 2002

Laying lines for the planting of a new willow bed, Walkers Farm, Stathe, 2000

Willow sets for planting

Planting willow, Walkers Farm, Stathe

One-year-old rods, 18ins in length, are planted leaving one-third above soil level

Mechanical harvesting with Ken Pimm, Ray Winchester and Ben Coles,
English Hurdle, Curload

Spiling, Langport, 2001 – the 'green' solution to waterside erosion problems

Spiling, Langport, 2001 – preparation of the river bank

Spiling, Darren Cooke 2002, English Hurdle, Curload

Musgroves

Willow Growers

The Musgroves have been involved in the cultivation of willow for some 50 years or more. The present business was set up after the Second World War by Arthur Musgrove, father of Les and grandfather of Mike who now run the family business together. Arthur initially cut willow trees for furniture making. Today, the family cultivates, harvests and sells high-quality willow. They have earned their reputation for good withies at a reasonable price and provide a caring 24-hour service. Second-class willow is sold for hurdle making. They have never needed to advertise, their reputation having spread far and wide.

The Musgroves' future looks good; 90 per cent of their regular customers are from other parts of the UK and orders have recently come in from Ireland and even as far afield as New Zealand. The path to success, as they see it, is to supply and produce a high-quality product. They do, however, feel strongly that businesses such as theirs should receive greater recognition and financial support. They are, after all, producing and selling a biodegradable and renewable material which can be used in a variety of ways. Growing is only part of the cycle. Finding new challenges and diverse outlets for willow is obviously the secret to success for the Somerset willow industry as a whole.

Les, Jack, Mike and Holly Musgrove at Lakewall, Westonzoyland, 2002

John Dye cuts willow by hand for Musgroves, Middle Moor, 2002

Mike Musgrove, Les Musgrove and John Dye loading willow, 2002

Les Musgrove

Mike and Les Musgrove with the harvested willow, Willow Fields, Lakewall, Westonzoyland

Mike, Holly, Jack and Les Musgrove with their ducks

Preparing a rose knot

Mike Musgrove uses a wooden mallet to even up the butt ends, 2001

Les and Mike Musgrove tie and bundle willow, 2001

A rose knot. E.M. and H.J. Lock (willow growers and contractors)

Brian Lock sorting willow, 2002

Brian Lock sorting willow prior to boiling, 2002

Stripped willow ready for distribution and sale, 2002

S. Alba Coerulea

Cricket-bat willow

One of the most specialised and exclusive commercial uses for willow today is in the making of handcrafted cricket bats. The wood is obtained from *S. Alba Coerulea* and only the female trees produce the necessary uniformity and quality. The species is favoured for the light, tough, springy, straight-grained, white wood that it produces.

The willow sets are grown from stools which are cropped every four years. Ground preparation, fencing and subsequent weeding, grass cutting or spraying are essential in order to prevent the young shoots being overrun with undergrowth during the first year of each cycle. Competition for light encourages the sets to grow straight and tall. Once cut the set is graded and, where possible, a clean stem of not less than 12ft, allowing 9ft 6ins of trunk and 2ft 6ins for planting, is obtained.

Sets are planted to a depth of 2ft 6ins. No staking is required but it is essential that rabbit guards are fitted. Spacing is 36ft apart in plantation form and 30ft apart in single rows. Maintenance is of paramount importance; trees neglected for even just one year during their lifetime have little or no commercial value. The side shoots can be rubbed off in the early stages to a height of 10ft, or if allowed to grow beyond this stage cut off flush with the bark in an upward direction. The best conditions in which to grow these sets are in good quality soil over clay, which is well drained but with a high water-table of between 18–30ins.

The average lifespan of a commercially grown tree is between 15 and 20 years. Cricket-bat willow trees are normally purchased standing, with all felling, extraction and clearing being the job of a willow specialist such as J.S. Wright & Sons Ltd. The trees are measured at 4ft 8ins from ground level with a minimum girth of 56ins and a clean trunk of 7ft. Each tree has to be replaced on a one-to-one basis.

Cricket and willow have a long shared history – the sport was first played during the fourteenth century, at which time bats were cut randomly from any variety of willow, thereby producing inconsistent results. English cricket-bat willow, the production of which is concentrated in Essex and Suffolk, is exported throughout the world. Climatic conditions in this region are ideal, although Australia and New Zealand are considering a programme for growing the species.

It could perhaps be argued that greater acknowledgement of companies such as Millichamp & Hall (handmade cricket-bat makers), J.S. Wright & Sons Ltd (willow specialists and merchants) and the Anglian Willow Service should be given by the world's top cricket players and the companies who sponsor these stars and the major cricket events.

Roderick Hector and George Wright at Aller Moor, Near Burrowbridge, 2002

Removing side shoots to assume a straight leader

Protecting the young cricket-bat willow (S. Alba Coerulea) is vital

George Wright measures the girth of S. Alba Coerulea *at 4ft 8ins from ground level*

Marking S. Alba Coerulea *for felling*

Millichamp & Hall

Handcrafted cricket-bat makers

My father, who thrust a bat into my hand almost as soon as I could walk, first fuelled my interest in cricket. I represented my school and local club, reaching county age group level and still turn out most weekends during the summer.

My first contact with Millichamp & Hall was as a customer and I quickly realised that there was something special about these bats that you did not find in others. At the time it was difficult to tell but, having been hand making them personally now for two years, [I know that] the secret is in the pressing, the shape of the handle and the weight distribution that you can only tailor-make by using traditional tools – draw knives, spoke shaves and rounded planes. There is nothing as satisfying as making a bat for a particular person in front of their eyes whilst ensuring that it has all the characteristics they are after.

Seeing the willow delivered in its raw state and shaped lovingly and then being able to go out and use it on an English summer's afternoon is for me a privilege that not many can enjoy. My only hope is that handmade bats continue to be crafted in the same way for years to come. It is no secret that the English-grown willow performs better than others due to the climate in this country and because particular attention is put into getting the most from each cleft.

(Nick Taylor)

Robert Chambers relates:

As if in complete contrast to my fellow colleague Nick, I hated cricket as a youngster. What a boring sport, all those hours standing about fielding only to be bowled out first ball at the crease (in my case anyway)!

My love for cricket was somewhat faked until recent years. Who would have thought I would end up owning a small company in Taunton, producing the thing that caused me so much embarrassment on the cricket field?

After leaving Haygrove School at 16 I embarked on a career in the Army. This definitely wasn't the life for me, so I left. After several months I found myself attending an interview for a mystery woodworking job. Imagine my surprise when I found out what the job entailed. The thought of making cricket bats certainly appealed to me though. I was told at the interview that only a handful of people make handmade cricket bats and opportunities like the one I was about to be offered were rare. The fact that the job was unusual and interesting, coupled with my passion for woodwork, prompted me to accept Millichamp & Hall's offer.

From an early age I can always remember my passion for wood. Both my father and grandfather were practically gifted in the fashioning of this most versatile material. I obviously acquired some of their skills and set about quickly proving my worth as a pod shaver. After a year's training I became a fully fledged bat maker, making bats for both the general public and top professionals alike. Four years after starting with Millichamp & Hall as an apprentice I had the opportunity to buy out the owners. This was a bold move on my part but one I will never regret. Now, after two years of owning and running Millichamp & Hall, I feel a great sense of achievement and hope to continue breathing life into this rare and interesting but now sadly dying trade.

One of the most frequent questions I'm asked is 'Don't you find this job boring, making the same old thing everyday?' People struggle to realise that each bat is a work of art, having its own very unique and individual characteristics. No two bats are ever the same, every day produces a new challenge and therefore I never get bored. Another great love of mine is customer relations, meeting interesting people, getting to know them and producing a tailor-made bat suited to their very own unique personality.

Seeing that person's eyes light up on delivery of their new cricket bat, and then sometimes even observing them score runs with it, produces a very warm glow inside.

Rob Chambers and Nick Taylor, The Willow Yard, Somerset Cricket Ground, Taunton, 2002

S. Alba Coerulea

The clefts are graded into various categories

Nick Taylor and Robert Chambers eye up cricket bats in the making

Handcrafted cricket bats made by Millichamp & Hall

The Somerset Willow Company

Three Generations of Willow Craftsmanship

Aubrey Hill was a carpenter and joiner by trade. His father worked as a basket maker for a company at North Petherton. Father and son set up a business together when Aubrey had completed his National Service. At first, they mainly fashioned pigeon and picnic baskets. Aubrey explains:

The reason we have stayed in business is that we are not afraid to move on to something new. Pigeon baskets died out when the railway stopped carrying livestock, then we had to find something else. We made hundreds of picnic baskets before competition killed it for us. Then we moved on to hot-air-balloon baskets and conservatory furniture. The market for these items has remained steady, although when foot and mouth stopped the balloons flying we realised that we needed something else. We were asked by a private individual, directed to us by Green Funerals at Watchet, for a willow coffin – which is nothing new really.

The Somerset Willow Company is the acknowledged number-one basket maker for Bristol-based Cameron Balloons. The chances are that if you see a hot-air balloon in flight it will probably be a Cameron balloon, from the world's foremost balloon and basket designers. The baskets are woven in Bridgwater from willow grown on the Somerset Levels.

As well as all this, Aubrey Hill and Darrell, his son, also specialise in furniture and undertake special commissions. They are recognised among the country's leading willow craftsmen. The company employs thirteen key staff, including nine fully trained basket makers who complete a minimum of five years' training.

The company traded as E.J. Hill & Son until the early 1990s, when Arthur Edwards, a furniture designer, joined the firm. It had always been his dream to make furniture with English willow and it was at his suggestion that the name of the company was changed to The Somerset Willow Company. Willow furniture is very much back in vogue, having a natural appeal with an ageless grace and refinement.

The company remains passionate about traditional craftsmanship, which means that every item, be it a balloon basket or a piece of furniture, is produced to the highest standard. An understanding of modern design and changing market trends plays an important role in ensuring that the West Country's leading manufacturer of willow-based products continues to go from strength to strength. The main backbone of the company lies with the production of balloon baskets and willow coffins, the latter of which helps to meet the growing environmental need for sustainability. After 35 years they continue to produce willow baskets for the ancient trade of mud-horse fishing which still continues at Stolford, a small hamlet north of Bridgwater.

Peter Woodberry, Tim Edmunds, Domenico Carrone, Andrew Hill, Karen Moule, Darrell Hill and Aubrey Hill, 2002

Domenico Carrone working on a balloon basket, The Somerset Willow Company

Andrew Hill, a willow coffin in the making

The Mud-Horse Fishermen

Mud-horse fishing must be one of the most extraordinary ways of making a living today, although the tradition is thought to have begun as far back as Roman times. Brendan Sellick's family have been fishing in this way for at least four generations. Brendan's great-grandfather had ten children and his grandfather had nine, the youngest of whom was Brendan's father; it seems that the role of the mud-horse fisherman fell to either the youngest or only son in the family.

There were once around a dozen such fishermen in the whole of the Bristol Channel, but this had dropped to just six or seven by the time that Brendan started in the 1950s. Numbers dwindled still further, until, by the late 1980s, he had become the last in the line of this dying breed. The fishermen traditionally had their own particular patches which were handed down or sold on, all of which represented an environment amidst the vast and dangerous local mudflats which to most would be intractable but which their skill and experienced enabled the mud-horse fisherment to negotiate.

The mud-horse, a simple device much like a table tipped upside-down with a nose piece, four legs and a platform to take the complete weight of the body, is propelled across the mud at great speeds, mostly by the feet of the fisherman. A mud-horse generally has to be replaced every 10–15 years and there are normally six to hand to allow for damage, or the occasional one being washed away.

At the time of writing, Brendan has not been fishing on the flats for about the last year and is more likely to be found cooking up brown shrimps and gutting fish in the nearby fish house at Stolford. The role of the mud-horse fisherman has now fallen to Adrian, Brendan's only son, who remembers taking his younger sister out in a 'willy' basket and allowing her to mess around in the puddles whilst her father and brother collected and sorted the day's catch. Adrian is now the last remaining mud-horse fisherman still working the mudflats of the Bristol Channel.

A century ago a branch of the Sellick family, who died out after the Second World War, moved to Cardiff Bay where, in the outlying district of Splott, they owned a shop. It was found that the mud-horse was not used as widely there; instead fishermen used the more stable flatner boats, made and sold in Bridgwater, which could be slid across the mud and through the shallow waters.

Mud-horse fishermen, Adrian and Cane Sellick, Stolford, 2002

The mud-horse is kept below the high-water mark and weighted with stones

Cane Sellick negotiates the pathway between the mud-flats

Adrian Sellick rides the mud-horse across the flats

The catch is emptied out into a sieve where the rubbish is sorted out

The shrimps are caught in the tapered end of shrimp nets

Brendan Sellick prepares the day's catch for sale, Stolford

Bruce Scott, Tony James, John Nash, 2002

Watchet Boat Museum

It all started in 1996 when a small group of Watchet sailing enthusiasts borrowed the last sailing flatner from the Somerset County Museum Service to publicise the idea of a Watchet Community Marina. They sailed the boat at the Festival of the Sea in Bristol that year and much enthusiasm was generated. Further boats were acquired and the Watchet Boat Museum was founded. It is sited in the Old Goods Shed, built for the original broad-gauge West Somerset Railway Company in 1862.

Flatners, or flatties, are usually defined as double-ended, flat-bottomed boats. They have no keel and the sides may be flat and single planked or clinker built. They are found all over the world but the museum concentrates on the Somerset flatners. They include turf boats, withy boats, bay boats and barges. Found on the peat moors of Somerset, the turf boats were used for carrying the cut and dried peat blocks to market and were towed manually from the bank, or propelled by means of a pole. Of simple and often crude construction, they have identical ends with simple planked sides. It is possible that these boats were originally a development of the log boats, with extended sides. Sizes tended to vary between 15ft and 19ft in length.

The withy boats were traditionally used on the Somerset Levels to carry the cut and bundled withies to the basket makers. The construction of vessels such as these is somewhat more sophisticated and looks more familiar to the modern eye, with the stem and the stern raking at different angles. The sides are either flat elm boards or clinker built. The boats were pulled along the banks of the many drainage ditches which cover the Somerset plain. It is thought that these vessels were a later development of the turf boat, although both were used as general farm transport before motor vehicles became common.

The river boats (19ft–20ft long) are of similar construction but the bottom is generally curved both ways into a long, narrow, pointed spoon shape to allow the boats to be launched down the sloping muddy banks of the local waterways, particularly the River Parrett. Used as fishing boats, they were rowed upstream with the incoming tide and salmon were 'dipped' out of the water with a large dip net. Since the 1950s many of these boats have been converted to carry an outboard engine. River boats are still sometimes used on the Parrett; over-fishing in the Atlantic has, however, reduced the work available for these boats.

Further development of the river boat led to the emergence of the Bay boat, which was used in Bridgwater Bay for fishing and for bringing coal and sheep from South Wales.

The barges were huge by comparison. Most commonly moored at Bridgwater, they were used for transporting coal to Taunton and Langport from the collieries. The barges were crewed by two men and a boy and were pulled along the towpath by a horse. That said, below Bridgwater these boats travelled up and down on the tide. With the arrival of the railways and the improvements in road transport the barges gradually fell out of use and none now remain.

Watchet Boat Museum

Mrs Cattle's old withy boat,
Bobbetts Meade, 2002

Ian Mayes with his double-ended
flatner boat Ostara

Woodspring Bay, North Somerset, 2002

The old withy yard, Stathe, 2002

Old withy yard interior, 2002

The varnishing room, old withy yard interior, 2002

Old withy yard interior, 2002

Floods on the A361 between Burrowbridge and Taunton, 1999

Willows act as landmarks in time of flood, 2000

The 'Willow Man' under reconstruction, 2001

Serena de la Hey with her assistant Lucy Watten, 2001

Ian Strugnell, 2000

Opposite: *Guy Martin, maker of contemporary furniture, Crown Studios, Crewkerne, 2002*

Peter Nicholas supervises the Willow Workshop at Hambridge School, 2002

Willow charcoal workshop with Kate Lynch at Hambridge School, 2002

Working with willow

Westonzoyland Pumping Station

Museum of Steam Power and Land Drainage

Westonzoyland was the first pumping station to be built to lift flood water from the Somerset Levels and Moors. In fact it is the only one to survive with the steam engine still working and the building intact. The station, which housed a beam engine and scoop-wheel to lift the water, was originally built in 1831 by the Middlezoy, Othery and Westonzoyland Drainage Board. Experience with the engine proved the benefits of mechanical drainage. Despite all this, in 1850, the year of disastrous flooding, it became apparent that a better system was required.

The present Easton and Amos drainage machine, incorporating a centrifugal pump, was installed in 1861. This engine was the first of eight similar installations on the Levels and remained in service until the adjacent diesel-engine pumping station was built in 1951. The old station was left derelict and fell into disrepair, but in 1977 a group of enthusiasts from the Somerset Industrial Archaeology Society, with the consent of Wessex Water, the owners of the site, restored the engine and ran it on an occasional basis for the general public. This group became the Westonzoyland Engine Trust, acquiring charitable status in 1980. It leased the station and most of the site from Wessex Water. In 1990 the Trust purchased the buildings and a major part of the site. Since that time they have rebuilt the 71ft chimney, stabilised the engine-house, rebuilt the pump-house and established a new exhibition space and refreshment area.

After a great deal of work the Trust obtained registration as a museum in 2002. Even in 2003 work continues on both the buildings and the growing collection of engines. It is interesting to note that all of the original buildings are now Grade II listed, a rare honour for secular structures.

The Westonzoyland Pumping Station is open for static displays every Sunday throughout the year from 2p.m. to 5p.m. Live steam displays are given on the first Sunday of each month from April to October and all bank holidays, including New Year's Day, but excluding Christmas Day and Boxing Day.

John Trenchard, Beryl Eaton, David Eaton and Andy Carter at Westonzoyland Pumping Station, 2002

Westonzoyland Pumping Station, 2002

Westhay Moor in flood, 2000

Flooded landscape, Common Moor, Hartlake

David Walker, Keeper of Social History at the Somerset Rural Life Museum, during the wassail celebrations, 2002

Somerset Rural Life Museum

Housed in the Victorian farmhouse and buildings of Abbey Farm and including the Home Barn of Glastonbury Abbey, the Somerset Rural Life Museum illustrates life in rural Somerset during the nineteenth and early-twentieth centuries, with displays of traditional farming practices and local industries such as peat cutting, withy growing, and cheese and cider making.

The farmhouse itself was built in the 1890s and now contains kitchen, dairy and washroom displays. In addition, the John Hodges Gallery display tells the life of a nineteenth-century farm labourer and his family. The orchard is planted with reference cider apple varieties and is home to beehives and rare breeds of sheep. The Abbey Barn was built in the fourteenth century for the 'home' manor of Glastonbury Abbey to store farm produce. The most striking feature is its roof. The medieval craftsmen created a system of two-tier cruck frames to support the weight of the stone tiles.

The museum, as part of Somerset County Museums Service, holds highly significant agricultural history collections. It opened in 1976 and has been supported from the outset by the Friends group, who manage the tea room and the shop, produce a newsletter, publish educational material and assist financially and in kind through conservation, documentation and research. School groups visit the museum for activities relating to the National Curriculum, and specialist associations such as art, photography and local-history groups all use the museum as a resource, as do individuals researching rural topics and family history. The museum's temporary exhibition gallery is in great demand by local artists and craftspeople.

David Walker is keeper of Social History at the Somerset Rural Life Museum:

We structure the programme of activities and events to learn from the past, to relate to the environment and to give old traditions a contemporary relevance. Every January 17th on Old Twelfth Night, we wassail our apple trees and burn an 'ashen faggot', a bundle of green ash wood tied with withies. These age-old customs are to ensure a successful new year with a good crop of apples.

The River Isle in the morning mist, 1998

Rush: 1998–2002

The True Bulrush
Scirpus lacustris

Each year towards the end of the summer, members of The Basket Makers Association meet to cut rush from the River Isle in Somerset. This sometimes involves wading waist deep into the river and at first glance, it could be mistaken for a scene in rural China, but it is part of the hidden life of the Somerset Levels.

Rush grows in streams and ponds and is harvested as a commercial crop in parts of England as well as on the Continent. It varies in size, quality and texture according to the area in which it is grown and the season. Usually about 6ft in height it has a round, emerald-green pithy stem when growing but this turns paler when dried. It has no leaf, just a silvery sheath at the butt or root end and a cluster of reddish-brown flowers at the tip. This, the true bulrush, is often mistaken for the Reedmace or false bulrush (*Typha lattifolia*) with its large bulbous brown head.

Rush is harvested when green and in England this is traditionally between the hay and corn harvest, during the summer. It is at its best from late June and throughout July depending on the weather. The clumps, or stands, are cut as close to the roots as possible and need to be handled carefully as they are brittle and easily damaged. The sap is then dried out either under cover or in the open air, a process which can take anything from a few days to about three weeks. Rush is best stored in a dark place and can be kept for several seasons, although it may become mouldy if it gets damp.

The qualities of the rush depend to a large extent on where the plant was originally grown. For example, freshwater rush from Portugal and Holland is long and soft, whilst Dutch saltwater rush is shorter and tends to be brown and hard. Yugoslavian rush, by contrast, is very hard and difficult to mellow and use.

Reedmace or False Bulrush
Typha lattifolia

The European flat rush or Reedmace is a good material for use in seating. It is greenish-brown in colour, semi-circular in section and hard in texture. The leaves, which are wide and flat and have a fleshy area at the base, can also be used successfully. This material wears well but is difficult to use for very fine coils. Reedmace can often be harvested free as it is prolific to the extent that it can rather overwhelm other vegetation.

The Basket Makers Association

This welcoming association includes professional basket makers as well as chair seaters, plus those who do it for enjoyment and those who are new to the craft. An interest in weaving baskets, seating chairs, experimenting with materials and researching methods has brought this varied group of makers together to share their skills and interests. Members are known to gather their materials from hedgerows, gardens and rivers and some even grow their own collection of willow in order to achieve a variety of bark and colour in their work and to preserve the diversity of the species. Several members teach basket making and chair seating. Membership of the group is open to anyone working in the field.

Belinda, Hannah, Matthew and Mark Humphry, 2002

Lorraine Houlden, rush cutting, 1998

Lorraine Houlden and Geoff Rice setting out in the leaky boat, 1998

Jennifer John, Caroline Brown, Hilary Burns and Jo Hynes with her children, 1998

It could almost be a scene in rural China, Jennifer John, 1999

Harvesting rush, 1998

Sook Shackleton and Hilary Burns, 2002

Philip Geers, Lorraine Houlden and Geoff Rice, 1998

Jo Hynes, 1998

Jo Hynes and Hilary Burns, 1998

Never too young, 1999

Linda Lemieux in her coracle, 2002

Christopher Amey and Lorraine Houlden, 1998

Bringing in the rush harvest, 1998

Hilary Burns, 1998

Graham Wilkinson evens up the butt ends of rush on the ground to produce a neat bundle, 2000

Jennifer John and Philip Geers sort the rush, 1998

Measuring and tying rush

Sook Shackleton and Sarah Pank, 1999

121

Lyn Edwards, 1999

Basket Makers South West, 1999

Lorraine Houlden, 1999

Rush

Modelling rush hats, 2002

One of Jill Wilkinson's gorgeous rush hats

Jo Hynes plaiting with rush

The bolts of rush are opened up and left to dry

Lorraine Houlden re-seats a chair with rush

The final piece

John Excell, The Cane Workshop at Hambridge, 2002

The Cane Workshop, 2002

View of Dundon Hill from Copley Wood, 1999

Reed: 1997–2002

Marsh Reed

Phragmites australis

Marsh reed grows extensively on marshlands and is abundant in wet places. Unrestricted flow of water onto and off reed beds is required for successful growth; reed does not favour stagnant water. These conditions are not particularly conducive to harvesting sedge and reed, but innovations in mechanisation now facilitate the control of the water-level by pumping. As such, mechanised cutters can be used when harvesting both these materials. Rhynes (ditches) need to be dredged to a width of 12ft and a depth of 4ft and in order to be effective water should be at least 2ft 6ins deep. Provided the reed bed is flooded for several months of the year, the benefits appear to be the same, whether the flood is in winter or early summer. High water reduces the invasion of weeds and stable conditions are very important. For greater yields a constantly high water-level is advantageous, although the ability to control the water-supply for harvesting and practicability is just as important. It is interesting to note that a reed bed consumes between 3ft and 5ft of water each year.

In the Netherlands reed is used to aid land reclamation; it is grown for a few years as a method of helping farmers drain and render their land fit for arable farming. Where reed has been cultivated for many years the ground is often firm and consolidated, whilst newly developed beds are commonly found on softer soil. On the Continent, reed beds are mainly sited on inorganic soil so that harvesting problems do not arise. Ditches are arranged so that water can be regulated – dry in winter to permit easy harvesting and wet in early summer.

Large coastal reed beds are often located at the back of salt marshes, where freshwater dilutes the sea water, as well as on low-lying ground near river beds. A high nutrient level is required in order for reed to thrive, which is simply not contained in either rain and spring water. The main salt marsh area in the UK is in East Anglia.

Reed is made up of an upright stem and a vertical rhizome (an underground rootlike stem that bears both roots and shoots). The stem later branches into two to three dozen reeds. Horizontal rhizomes grow each year by 2ft–6ft before bending up to become new vertical rhizomes. Reed varies in length and quality, depending on genetic differences as well as variations in the soil and water regime. Plants derived from one seed form a clone.

Propagation can be achieved by growing reed from seed (which requires expert knowledge) or by digging old reed in late winter and cutting the rhizomes well below soil level. These can produce no less than 11 yards of rhizomes and 45 reeds in the second year. Shoots grow faster earlier in the year and in warmer weather which means that a hot spell in May will have more effect than one in July, and a hot summer will give longer reeds. Flowering is usually in late August and September, with the fruits ripening in November. Harvesting starts in late December or January and continues until the following April. Once harvested, the reeds are bound together in bundles, which are stacked to dry for five months – before it is used as a thatching material it must be dried and hardened. As the reed dries it shrinks in width. Reed is sold in bundles, a standard unit being 24ins in circumference measured 12ins from the butt. (A 'fathom' was six standard bundles, measuring 6ft in circumference.)

Sedge, a flexible and durable thatching material used only for ridging today, was traditionally measured in scores – one score being 20 bundles or bunches. There were 600 bunches in a load or 100 fathoms.

135

Setting up stooks, Compton Dundon, 2000

Richard Wright, 2002

Thatching

The thatcher is a Master Craftsman. The word 'thatch' originates from the Saxon 'thaes', meaning roofing. A wide variety of materials, including reed, straw, bracken, turf and heather were once all used for church, cottage, haystack, manor or pigsty alike, as evidence from excavated Neolithic sites has revealed. Later, humbler dwellings continued to be thatched with wheat or water reed, whilst newer roofing materials were used on higher status buildings and so displaced the more traditional thatched roof of the earlier days.

In the West Country the most acceptable thatching material has long been wheat reed; consequently combed wheat straw is still grown by a limited number of farmers to meet the demand. The future of the thatcher's essential material will depend on its continued availability. The crop is traditionally harvested by a binder when the straw is at its peak – before the wheat ripens – usually around late July or early August. It is then stooked to dry naturally. These stooks mark the last stage of the traditional harvest. The rows run from north to south to allow even exposure to the sun, with 10–12 sheaves leaning against one another. The leaf of the straw is then combed by a reed-combing machine which is attached to a threshing machine. Before the days of mechanisation combing wheat would have been done by hand and was a tedious job most often carried out by women. By mid-June every thatcher should have sufficient reed to meet his needs for the following year.

Thatching is a highly physical occupation, which incorporates no mechanisation. Furthermore, many thatchers prefer to work alone. The thatching material is laid vertically from eaves to ridge in widths of 2ft–3ft, working from right to left. After positioning the thatching material, the base end is stoked and coaxed, tapped and dressed by knocking the ends with a leggett (a square board with a handle). The bundle is secured with hazel or willow spars (pegs) which are made using a method that has remained unaltered for centuries. A thatcher's saying proclaims 'that which grows in the wet, lasts longer in the wet', and, indeed, willow spars outlive hazel in wet thatch. This may have something to do with the constituent aspirin found in willow which deters woodworm from boring holes in the spars.

The only bundles of reed to be laid horizontally are those which form the ridge roll, which gives pitch to the roof and a solid foundation into which the pegs bite. The top is then finished with a pattern and quite often includes a sculpture that identifies the work of a particular thatcher.

Before starting to re-thatch, it is usual to remove the previous layer. In some cases the roof rafters may need renewing or require treatment for woodworm or decay. If the roof was originally straw-thatched, the existing thatch has to be completely removed and all necessary repairs made to the rafters. The addition of tilting fillets to all eaves, barges and windows is necessary to create the required tension. When renewing or re-thatching a roof with water-reed the thatcher needs to do very little in terms of working on the roof structure beyond moderate repairs to the timbers and chimney stacks.

The chosen method of thatching should be in keeping with the character of the property. Although more expensive than tiles, a roof thatched by a skilled thatcher in East Anglia should last approximately 80 years if Norfolk reed is used. In the West Country, where the pitch of the roof is generally less, this time may be substantially shortened.

Reed grown in this country is considered by some to be better suited to our climate, but as supplies of British reed have dwindled other reed-producing countries have recognised the potential of the British market. Perhaps the time has come to restore the British reed beds and in the process protect and nurture the wildlife that depends on this environment.

Stooks mark the final stage of the traditional harvest

D.C. Wright

Thatching Contractor

Harold Wright was born at Hurst Cottage, Compton Dundon, a thatched dwelling which adjoins a working dairy farm. The Wrights have been farming this area for over 200 years and it has been said that 'they always grew a bit of wheat and their own kit to do the binding [but] you wouldn't get a new one today.' In 2003 the family rents 20 acres across from Millway Farm and has 11 acres down at Hayes.

When Harold left school he joined his father, William, in the family business. As thatchers and spar makers they served the surrounding farms and in 1925 bought Rose Cottage, more commonly known today as Thatchers Yard.

Harold first met his wife Marjorie whilst on embarkation leave before being posted overseas to join the Second Division Cameronion Scottish Rifles. He served two-and-a-half years in India, Burma, Malaysia and Singapore. Six months after he returned from the war the couple were married.

William died aged 63, leaving two sons to continue the business. Dennis, Harold's youngest son, joined his father when he left school and Richard joined the family business some time later. As the Wrights know all too well, simply growing wheat for its grain value would not be profitable; the value of reed is much higher.

The Wright family, Millway Farm, Compton Dundon, 2002

David Wright, Tom Rymer, Andrew Wright and George Willis hauling in the wheat reed, 2002

Tom Rymer, 2002

A wheat-reed stack, as opposed to a haystack, is called a 'mow'

Reed-combing, 1997

Reed-combing, 1997

Reed-combing, 2001

George Willis, 1997

Charlie, the thatcher's mate

Reed-combing, 1997

Martin Dunster, 2001

Dennis Wright and Martin Dunster, 2001

Dennis Wright, 2001

Dennis Wright, Butleigh Wooton, 2001

The most accepted thatching material in the West Country is wheat reed

A leggett (a square board on a handle) is used to stoke, coax, tap and dress the base ends of the thatching material

Knee pads as well as palm straps are worn for protection

The bundle is secured with willow or hazel spars or pegs

The thatching material is laid vertically, working from right to left

Split strips of spar material are used in a decorative manner at the ridge

Willow spars outlive hazel in wet thatch, hence the adage 'that which grows in the wet, lasts longer in the wet'

Harold Wright sits astride his spar stool, cutting willow to length and then splitting it using a large knife, Thatchers Yard, Compton Dundon, 1997

Holnicote Thatching Project, Selworthy

In 2000 a three-year thatching project began at Holnicote, an estate given to the National Trust by the Acland family in 1944 which constituted the biggest single gift ever received by the organisation. The project came about in 1999 following a survey of the thatched roofs on the estate, the results of which revealed that many were in need of repair. This provided a unique opportunity to start a repair programme and to begin research aimed at gaining a better understanding of the performance of thatch and thatching techniques. In addition the project was also designed to assess the viability of producing appropriate materials on the estate such as thatching reed, as well as willow and hazel for coppicing and thatching spars.

Master thatcher Keith Payne helped to initiate the project as well as train an apprentice thatcher. Daniel Bishop, who at the time of writing is part of the direct National Trust labour force. Daniel should become one of the most highly qualified thatchers and in the future could serve as a trained consultant for the 'Trust', making this a highly cost-effective venture. Keith Payne felt that it was important to conserve the vernacular style which has been used for several hundred years.

Through successful implementation the project is enabling tenant farmers to farm in a sympathetic manner, carefully balancing their need to make a living with concerns for the local environment. Many have actively participated by producing suitable varieties of wheat reed for thatching, the first harvest of which was in 2001. Through projects such as this, the National Trust is in a unique position to proactively encourage an environmentally-sustainable approach to the management of land and buildings.

To celebrate Japan 2001 a Japanese Minka was constructed at Kew Gardens in London and Keith Payne was contracted to undertake the project. The roofing materials used were Scottish water reed, bamboo for the supports and ties made from flax. When the roof needs re-thatching in the future it is hoped that *miscanthus* (the usual material used in the Far East) will be used, having been grown and cultivated in the UK. *Miscanthus*, which can be produced competitively and can also be used for biomass, is considered a good alternative to the imported foreign water reed but not as a suitable replacement for the indigenous materials.

Daniel Bishop, apprentice thatcher, Bossington, 2002

Keith Payne uses local Porlock reed on Gibraltar Cottages, Porlock Weir, 1985 © K. PAYNE

Keith Payne, 'Japan 2001', Kew Gardens, London © K. PAYNE

Former Estate Manager for Porlock Manor Ben Hammett, with Royston Binding and Paul Biddiscombe, 2002

Richard Fryer uses foreign water reed to re-thatch 'The Orchard' at Dinnington, 2002

View of Glastonbury from the Tor

Richard and Henry Lang

'Second Prize Silver Lapwing Award (Farmcare FWAG)'

Home Farm is a family-run, 1,000-acre largely arable enterprise with winter wheat as the main crop plus winter rape, beans and linseed. In all 250 ewes (including 30 pedigree Dorset Down) graze in the paddocks and newly restored cider orchards. Countryside Stewardship Schemes have helped brothers Richard and Henry Lang to achieve a great deal of conservation work in a short space of time but their knowledge, commitment and hard work go well beyond the confines of the scheme. For example, the traditional management of their hay meadows and creation or reinstatement of several ponds are indicative of their long-term dedication to farming. In the last few years over 6,000 native broad-leaf trees have been planted, doubling the acreage of woodland on the farm, and three orchards have been restored. Set-aside land has been used positively: permanent grass areas have been established both to buffer sensitive habitats and provide suitable conditions for small mammals which feed local predators, in particular their resident barn owls. Rotational set-aside land is grown under the wild bird cover option to provide winter food for small birds.

Richard and Henry Lang use integrated crop management techniques wherever possible (during spring and summer no insecticides are used on the headlands – unploughed strips of land, which allow machinery to pass along). They also carefully maintain and restore hedging and field margins to encourage wildlife. Their 35 miles of hedgerows are sympathetically managed and over 4,920ft have been restored by laying and replanting. As a result of their hard work, grey partridges, brown hares and skylarks now frequent the farm.

Redundant dairy farm buildings have been carefully converted into a smokery, shop, restaurant and offices – all of which create local employment opportunities.

Silver Lapwing awards are presented annually to farmers who make the greatest contribution to conservation. Henry Lang points out, this doesn't always need to be judged in financial terms: 'much of our conservation work demands time and thought rather than money.'

Henry and Richard Lang, Home Farm, Curry Rivel, 2002

The growing of willow and miscanthus *as an energy grass has been widely encouraged*

Miscanthus *is considered a good alternative to the importation of foreign water reed*

Wheat reed

Water reed, Phragmites australis

Nigel Day, Reed Merchant

Force of circumstance and redundancy combined to encourage Nigel Day and his father, Mac, to set up their own business as reed suppliers in 1993. Both father and son, as well as Nigel's grandfather Alfred before them, had worked for Paul & Son, a reed merchant business which had been operating since 1832. The business of 2003 continues to be run from the same site at Manor Farm in Martock.

Most of the water reed used in the UK is imported from Hungary and Turkey where labour costs are low because of the employment of peasant workers. The quality of the water reed is medium to good depending on texture, tapering and size. The retail price of water reed, at the time of writing, is £1.40 per 60cm (almost 2ft) bundle and £140.00 for a bale (one bale is made up of 100 bundles). Mac remembers when wheat reed was £8 per ton in the 1940s, whereas today it is worth £600 a ton.

Water reed has a longer storage life than wheat reed, which is vulnerable to rats and mice and is more sensitive to storage conditions. Nigel forsees a bleak future for the industry because of the fall in the levels of wheat-straw production, a situation which is sometimes worsened by poor weather. He feels that there is a need for more growers working 15–20 acres rather than half a dozen big suppliers.

It is a very labour-intensive exercise, but one where the employment of old conventional methods is really the only way to achieve quality results. Adjustments can be made to suit but at the end of the day it comes down to the job being done in a caring manner with some thought. However, the future for the thatcher is still bright, although there is certainly an ongoing need for integrity and commitment.

Nigel and Mac Day, Manor Farm, Martock, 2002

Gerry Masters, Kota Mama

There are those who believe that a certain amount of trading took place between South America and Africa three millennia ago and recent discoveries of cocaine and tobacco within Egyptian mummies lend some credence to this theory. Journeys such as that undertaken in 1947 by Thor Heyerdhal with his *Kon-Tiki* boat constructed by South American Indians using reed and balsa, and much more recently the SES Expeditions led by John Blashford Snell down various water systems of South America, are still being made to demonstrate the possibility of ocean traffic between the continents in ages past. The boats used by the SES are built with reeds from Lake Titicaca and several other expeditions are being planned to test the theory in the Pacific, one group using the same boat builders as the SES. Gerry Masters, whilst working on the three Kota Mama expeditions, made discoveries and observations which led him to believe that it was actually the Durotriges in Somerset who first took the craft of building with reeds to South America!

On his return from South America in 1998 Gerry set about gathering rush from the River Yeo. However, the species proved too soft for satisfactory boat building and too difficult to dry so he looked around for another material. Water reed seemed to be a possibility and Gerry knew of a good supply out along the River Cam at its junction with the Yeo. He collected a useful amount and stored the reed in his garage.

His second attempt at a boat was still a little too small for comfort so a third was built, recycling the materials from the first two prototypes; the vessel was beginning to take on the form of a Russian doll with a boat inside a boat and so on! The third craft seemed to supply enough buoyancy to support Gerry's weight but was still unstable; a problem which was rectified with the addition of two small outriggers.

On 23 March 2002 Gerry launched *Kota Mama Six and Seven Eighths* (his hat size) at the Ilchester road bridge to the cheers and applause of residents of the town. With television camera crews, journalists and photographers from the newspapers looking on, and Rod Stewart's dulcet tones blasting out 'Maggie May' (it was supposed to be 'We are Sailing'), he set off on his epic journey; his final goal being the Second World War barrage balloon hanger at Pawlett. A further trip took place in August 2002, Gerry sailing his reed boat from Lechlade in Gloucestershire to Gravesend in Kent, a 160-mile journey, as a result of which over £3,000 was raised for charity.

If his theory is correct – and he is sure that it is – Gerry should be able to achieve the next stage of his dream: to build a larger boat that will carry him further down the Bristol Channel on the tide, then slide downhill to South America. He says he hasn't yet planned out how he will get back, but he's working on it.

Gerry Masters with his grandchildren, Victoria and David

Gerry Masters and his grandson David launch a reed boat, Ilchester, 2002

Pols Heath, Westhay

'New Lease of life for Levels peat sites'

In 2003 restoration projects are well under way to convert redundant peat-extraction sites at Pols Heath near Westhay into rich wildlife habitat. E.J. Godwin is working closely with the local environmental consultancy firm Terraqueous Ltd to pilot new strategies that will combine both environmental and commercial elements. The potential of this scheme is highlighted by the fact that a conservation reed bed recently established on a nearby peat-extraction site has now been designated as an SSI (Site of Special Scientific Interest).

Godwin's is a family-run business and, unlike larger producers elsewhere in the country, does not support the practice of working a site and then disposing of it in order to move on. Instead they seek to retain ownership and management of the worked land to recreate it as a valuable resource in its own right. By adopting this policy they are giving back to the social economy and wildlife. Reed production is a sustainable wetland industry which is also recognised for its conservation after-use. It has been estimated that Somerset alone imports approximately 400,000 bundles of reed per year for thatching purposes, much of which comes from Eastern Europe. It is anticipated that the yield from the Pols Heath site will be in the region of 1,000 bundles per hectare. (The site currently covers approximately 12 hectares.) Clay exposed by peat extraction has been utilised to construct water-retaining features around the site, structures which will be used with sluices to facilitate the careful water-level management that is required. Commercial beds of saw sedge have been similarly constructed and reed beds and lakes have been built purely for conservation purposes.

Ben Malin is responsible for developing economically and environmentally sustainable after-use strategies. It is hoped that the combination of conservation sites and commercial reed and sedge beds will form a model which can be repeated elsewhere on the Somerset Levels. In turn, this may also form the basis for peat-land restoration projects elsewhere in the country.

Ben Malin (Terraqueous Ltd), Graham Mitchell (Loglogic), Richard Bradford (LAMP), Marcus Frankpitt (Loglogic), Sally Mills (RSPB), Melvin Yeandle (English Nature) and Jonathan Coate (P.H. Coate & Son) with the new soft-track machine, Shapwick, 2002

RSPB, Ham Wall Nature Reserve

The RSPB relies on volunteers to undertake many different tasks. It is a charity that takes action on behalf of wild birds and the environment with a strong interest in conserving all biodiversity. It is the largest conservation charity in Europe, a great deal of whose work is concerned with acquiring and managing nature reserves which cover more than 100,000 hectares.

Ham Wall is one of the newest reserves, situated a couple of miles west of Glastonbury in Somerset. Habitat creation and husbandry play a large part in the work carried out on the site and tasks include restoration of wetland and management of grassland. Much of the British wetland wildlife faces a difficult battle against drainage and loss of habitat. At the time of writing, English Nature is actively encouraging landowners who participate in the Countryside Stewardship Scheme to take up the growing of reed as a wildlife-friendly and financially attractive alternative to pump-drained agriculture. Surveying and monitoring the wildlife and habitat is a fundamental part of the work and those with specialist natural history knowledge are needed to increase our awareness of the country's wildlife. Open days, talks and fund-raising events play an important part in the dissemination of information.

A case in point is the bittern – a mysterious and elusive bird which relies on the wetlands and spends much of its time in the reed beds. There are 2003 now between 10 and 20 males left in this country. Similarly, the water vole, once a common sight in our watercourses, is also threatened with extinction, a state of affairs which is the result of the combined threats posed by a decline in habitat alongside the increase of pollution and the American mink. The otter, a large wetland mammal, is also threatened by habitat loss, pollution and the increase of rural roads.

The aims of the RSPB are to create a wetland paradise of national and international importance where wildlife is protected and local people and visitors can learn about and experience a unique landscape.

RSPB volunteers, Ham Wall Reserve, 2002

Westhay Moor, a peat-extraction site

Mike Johnson holds an empty seed tray, Ham Wall Reserve, 2002

Preparing the polytunnel for reed propagation, 2002

Volunteers prepare seed heads for propagation, 2002

Moisture provides the necessary humidity for reed seedlings

A manual pump is used to fill the polytunnel with the required amount of water

Comfrey makes a very useful fertiliser

Comfrey has a very unpleasant smell

183

Trays of reed seedlings are over-wintered in purpose-made ponds

Reed ready for planting out

The planting of reed takes place in the spring

Bedding out reed, Ham Wall Reserve, 2002

Reed can be used for reclamation purposes

Watery landscape, as in times past

Reed is cut with a suitable machine

Reed beds provide a wonderful wildlife habitat

Burning is necessary to leave the bed clean for the next year's growth

Clearing the cut reed

Rhizomes are dug in late winter for replanting

Street Heath, 1999

Peat extraction, Street Heath, 1999

A wind pump is necessary to assist in regulating water levels

A watery nest, 2000

A Somerset rhyne bordered by willow trees and yellow iris at Aller Moor near Wedmore

Carymoor Environmental Trust

'Education by Demonstration'

In 1996 the vision of turning a restored landfill site in a tranquil corner of Somerset into a wildlife site to educate people about pollution and protection of the environment seemed a tall order. A group of enthusiasts were determined to surmount all obstacles and, with the support of the local landfill company, Wyvern Waste Services, they did achieve their dream. Along the way the programme gained momentum and has since become a nationally prominent project.

Volunteers work alongside academics to develop a 100-acre site of degraded land to achieve a living patchwork of habitats. Universities and respected national wildlife charities have become involved in the design and realisation of research projects to increase biodiversity on this site, which was formerly a munitions store during the Second World War. Some features dating from that time remain and are woven into the bigger picture of providing shelter for endangered species.

Whilst ecological restoration and development of the green environment are key aims here, there is another theme emerging at Carymoor demanding serious attention: demonstration of suitable development of the built environment. A site that hosts visits from school parties most days of the year and encourages adult groups with specialist or general interest needs a building to allow instruction to take place in an inspirational setting. As such, the visitor centre that was built to fill these requirements is timber-framed with lime-plastered walls, making use of medieval techniques and locally sourced new and reclaimed materials. Designed around the exciting concept of low environmental impact, the centre includes unusual features such as stilts on minimal foundations (creating a space beneath the building for rainwater storage), insulation provided by recycled newspapers, a sanitation system incorporating a compost chamber and a dedicated reed bed with its own 'discharge consent'. Tiles were used from a nearby demolished barn, doors were rescued from Victorian schools and the heating is generated from waste wood. The internal features include a high vaulted ceiling with exposed beams and a woven withy wall.

Carymoor is sited on the very edge of the Somerset Levels. Throughout the building and its surrounding grounds, willow is incorporated as a building material. Other natural materials used here include straw (in the unique lozenge-shaped straw-bale house with its living turf roof), reed, lime and sustainable softwoods such as Douglas Fir. Coppiced material from the immediate area forms the structure of a replica Bronze-Age roundhouse, which offers shelter on the extended ramble around the emerging and existing habitats. The entire site is boosted by solar and wind power.

Plans include the establishment of 24 acres dedicated to short-rotation coppice, willow and similar species for the provision of biomass material to create energy, craft materials and as experimentation in low-intensity planting regimes to benefit wildlife.

Taking 'education by demonstration' as its aim, and commitment to realistic protection of the environment as its ideal, Carymoor offers a chance for all to participate in defining and defending the important qualities of our landscape, incorporating the crafts and species we have inherited into a dynamic programme to inspire and support future custodians of the land.

Jill Gilbert (Executive Director) and Hamish Craig (Chairman), Carymoor, 2002

Amazon Nails

Barbara Jones 'Building with straw bales'

Straw is a by-product of wheat. One of the biggest attributes of straw-bale buildings its capacity for creative fun and the high level of involvement from the people who use and inhabit them. Building with bales can be inspiring and Barbara Jones, who is an exceptional teacher, works with groups of people who want to build their own dream homes. She believes that it is one of the most empowering experiences we can have.

Partly due to its insulation value and partly because of its organic nature, a straw-bale house feels very different inside. Once a person has decided how they want the structure to look and feel internally, they can imagine their ideal space and work within the practical limitations of the bales to see their dreams realised.

Barbara Jones has over 20 years of experience in building construction as a roofer and joiner. She has run her own all-women business, Amazon Nails in Todmorden, Yorkshire, since 1989. She built her first straw-bale building in 1994 and in the following year was awarded a Winston Churchill Fellowship, spending three months in the USA and Canada researching the process and gaining further practical experience. She has spent time with many of the most experienced builders and practitioners in America and Europe and is familiar with all of the most recent innovations that have arisen during the present exciting resurgence of sustainable building. Her skills lie in a comprehensive grasp of twentieth-century building practices and a knowledge of traditional skills such as lime-plastering, natural-clay plastering and cob-building. In 1998 she won a Queen Elizabeth Scholarship to increase her knowledge and skills in lime- and mud-plastering and cob-building. She was also awarded a Wingate Scholarship to conduct research into the movement of moisture in straw-bale walls.

Since 1995 she has been running an information and advice service from her office in Todmorden and has taught self-build courses all over Ireland and England. She has been involved in over 30 permanent structures and many more temporary ones. In Ireland, over the period 2000–01, she worked on Europe's first two-storey load-bearing straw-bale house, which was built in the shape of a spiral. The breadth of her experience speaks for itself. She is constantly in demand for consultancy, advice, work training and practical help. Her approach is simple and straightforward – a refreshing change from the complexities of modern life.

The straw-bale house at the Carymoor Environmental Centre was designed by Barbara. Its straw-bale walls are mounted on a base of recycled tyres stuffed with local clay and the roof has living turf insulated with fleece from British sheep. The lozenge-shaped house is used as a demonstration area and extends the centre's range of sustainable buildings. It imparts the message of low environmental impact development.

Barbara Jones, Carymoor, 2002

Two-day introductory course in straw-bale building, Carymoor, 2002

Preparing the necessary materials

Barbara Jones lays the first bale

Pinning starts from the fourth course with hazel pins, two per bale

Raising the roof plate

Knocking the bales back into shape

Bill Poirrier, artist and blacksmith

Tristan Elki

Load-bearing style straw bale; the bales take the weight of the roof

The roof plate is fastened to the foundations and the bales, and the roof is constructed above this

The ideal finishes for straw are traditional lime-based plasters or natural clay
plasters because of their breathable nature

*High plinth walls, self-draining foundations and large overhangs to the roof
are important design features*

A straw-bale building feels unique

Members of the Basket Makers Association

Philip Geers
3 April 1923–14 January 2003

Lorraine Houlden

Graham Wilkinson

Jennifer John

Hilary Burns

Lyn Edwards

John Excell

Sarah Pank

Philip Alfred Geers

3 April 1923–14 January 2003

Philip Geers qualified as an architect at the London Polytechnic, now the University of Westminster. Whilst pursuing this profession he spent eight years from 1953 to 1961 in Tanganyika. His second assignment, a period of two years from 1961 to 1963 in Kuwait, involved the building of the National Airport, whilst a further period, between 1963 and 1965 in Malawi, was spent working for a large multinational company.

In 1975 Philip and his wife June decided to 'drop out' in order to fulfil a dream that involved their love for the land. They joined a commune at Pilsdon in Dorset and it was there that Philip was first introduced to chair seating. It was, however, only when they left Pilsdon for Hambridge in Somerset that he began to experiment and in his own words 'taught himself from a book without the need for anyone looking over his shoulder.' He made several seats before he felt that he was getting somewhere.

Whilst living here at Hambridge, he discovered the rush found in the River Isle. This led to Philip fathering the beginnings of the 'rush cutting' which continues to this day. Rush harvesting first took place in 1976 at Earnshill, Hambridge, near Webbs Bridge. It was some years later that Philip negotiated the present arrangement with Mark Humphry's late father, the tenant of Manor Farm at Isle Abbotts.

Philip and his wife eventually purchased Turkey Cottage at Curload near Stoke St Gregory, where they became well-loved and respected members of the local community. Here he was able to pass on to others his knowledge and the sense of community which had drawn him to the countryside in the first place. Due to ill health in 2002, Philip handed over his role as 'leader' of this unique group to two fellow members, thereby securing the future of this band of traditional rush cutters in Somerset. Philip Geers died peacefully in Musgrove Park Hospital on 14 January 2003.

Lorraine Houlden, Rush and Cane

'Why do I do what I do?' This is a question Caroline asked of me some months ago when Christmas was approaching and it was a timely one. We are all victims of commercial spending whether we like it or not and a lot of thought and energy is put into meeting a special deadline. The presents we give are gratefully received and have use in the short term... but what about the long term? And there, in many ways, lies the answer to why I do what I do.

My hands are my tools plus a simple wooden cooking spatula, a pair of scissors and an old crotchet hook – and of course a hook for cutting the rush at harvest time. There is nothing more rewarding than seating a chair that may have been in someone's family for a very long time; through my work I am able to give it a future. The delight I feel when someone says to me 'I know this chair has no value in terms of money but this was my mother's chair and it brings back wonderful memories of her' or 'as a child I remember my father sitting on that chair in the study'. Most of the chairs I work on have strong sentiments attached to them and in a small way I am not only carrying on a tradition but I am preserving happy memories for other people.

The craft has been in existence for centuries and I hope will continue for many more centuries to come. Yes, it is hard work, and yes, I sport blisters and chaps, especially during the winter months. Not only is the end result rewarding, but I have also met some wonderful people along the way. To me my craft is simplicity at its best.

Graham Wilkinson, Rush and Cane

Jennifer John, Rush and Cane

After a career which included many years in mechanical engineering and further education in parts of the country from the Midlands to London, Graham Wilkinson moved with his wife Gill to West Dorset at the end of the 1970s.

A general interest in chairs was born after a handful of auction sale purchases, and then a friend asked Graham for some help in getting a dining chair cane panel repaired. He decided to have a shot at it himself and with the aid of a little Dryad Press booklet managed a reasonable result. This modest success triggered his concentration on chair seating.

In the early 1980s he managed to buy a redundant unmanned telephone exchange in the village where he and his wife live. He converted this into a workshop and started the business of chair repairs and re-seating stools and chairs using cane and seagrass. Again, he taught himself the seagrass skills and also attended a short course in furniture restoration at COSIRA in Salisbury.

Business developed along these lines for a few years before Graham added rush seating to his repertoire following tuition from John Excell. The rushes used in those days and for some years to come were imported by John from Holland.

In the late 1990s, Graham met Jennifer John at the Winsham Street Fair and subsequently Philip Geers invited him to join the rush cutters at Isle Brewers in July. Ever since he has been using these locally grown and harvested rushes. Latterly, his wife Gill has joined the rush-cutting group and she has started using the rushes to make country hats which she now sells.

I came to chair bottoming after buying two bedroom chairs which needed repairing and re-seating in cane. When I found out how much it would cost I decided I'd rather have a go myself. But how to do it? I signed on for a weekend course in cane seating at West Dean College near Chichester. I derived a lot of satisfaction from this and signed on for another weekend doing rush seating. From then on I bought up chairs and stools and sold them at fêtes and craft fairs. From this came enquiries for repairs. I didn't take on anything too grand as I was still learning, but people seemed happy with my work and more came in. At that time I was only doing it on a part-time basis to fit in with my other work as a part-time attendant at the Farm Museum at Botley in Hampshire.

When I moved to Somerset in 1986 I carried on doing chairs combined with car-boot sales, and antique and bric-a-brac stalls. Eventually, lifting heavy boxes became too much and I decided to concentrate solely on the chairs. When Philip Geers' phoned me and asked whether I would be interested in cutting my own rush I was delighted and have been cutting on the River Isle ever since. Customers seem genuinely interested to hear that a good old English chair has been re-seated as it would have been done originally.

Hilary Burns, Basket Maker

What is it about watching a basket maker work that is so fascinating? Is it that ancient connection to nature, the magic of turning a bundle of sticks into something beautiful and useful? I came to basket making through a background of fabric weaving, having trained at art school. Whilst living in London and working at the Central School of Art and Design in the 1980s, I joined the one-day-a-week City and Guilds course in Creative Basketry which was then running at the London College of Furniture. After completing the four years there was no turning back. I was fascinated by the multitude of methods by which baskets and other materials could be linked together to form a structure. At that time basket making was not fashionable and there was a general lack of regard for its value as a craft. Since then there has been a renewal of interest in basket-making techniques, which have been translated and transformed using a variety of unlikely materials which have found their way into the applied-arts departments of modern colleges.

My first tutors were Barbara Maynard and Lois Walpole, the traditional and contemporary sides of the coin. Barbara had started the Basket Makers Association in 1975 and from an initial handful of people it now boasts 900 members. It has provided a point of contact for many basket makers who were, in the early days of its existence, few and far between. The association also organised courses taught by older makers whose accumulated knowledge and skills had mainly been passed on without written instructions, and were thus in danger of being lost. Later I joined the committee and was their honorary secretary for three years. With interest in the craft growing in many areas of the country I helped to set up our local group Basket Makers South West. In my early basketwork I used untraditional recycled materials, plastic, wire and laminates, but since moving to Devon in 1985 my interest has grown in plant materials; willow, hedgerow and rush. The annual cycle of growth and harvest is a great grounding influence. I am growing many varieties of willow on my plot, trialling the crop to see which ones do well in the area and suit my method of making. Rush cutting is a highlight in the year's calendar. Not being a seater of chairs I use it for children's workshops. They love its silky surface, and the soft spongy structure is a good working material for smaller fingers.

Whenever basket makers meet they talk about the rigours of making a living from the craft. There is teaching of course, in order to continue passing on skills. But the question is how to achieve a balance; it's easy to take on too much and any hope of getting a flow of work goes out of the window. I'm not a maker with a standard range, although making a batch of several of one thing is good for honing skills. Hands get to 'know' the form and work gets better. Not naturally neat, I need constant practice. It's a 'slow' craft with a humble profile and generally a low perceived value. It takes an age to achieve speed and perfection. All of this accounts for the small numbers of those who take it up as a profession and the numbers of potential basket makers who reluctantly give it up for more lucrative ways of earning a living.

Recently more unusual commissions have turned up for me, showing a possible way forward. In a world of large businesses I make my living on a much smaller scale, weaving both functional and sculptural pieces, demonstrating and teaching, selling my work through the Devon Guild of Craftsmen at fairs and receiving commissions through word of mouth and lately the web. Basketry does not easily sustain the mark-up of shops and galleries and selling a large percentage of my work direct to the buyer is essential for me. Working from home as a self-employed craft worker has also had to fit around family life and three children.

Is there still a need or a place for baskets and makers or is this a craft in jeopardy of dying out? The tide may be turning. Industry and agriculture no longer operate on a scale that utilises baskets, begging the question 'is their place only as romantic relics of the past?' Changing times mean that baskets are beginning to be appreciated and paid for by those who recognise the skill and love the craft. We have a long way to go but increasingly as we have to address environmental concerns, a re-evaluation of skills and the importance of sustainability is taking place. If we want to reduce waste and packaging and can learn to be, or are forced to be less greedy, possibly then there could be a place for small-scale workshops, regional centres, the production of functional baskets from local materials, as well as a niche for the work of the artist/basket maker.

Lyn Edwards, Basket Maker

I was introduced to rush cutting by friend and fellow basket maker, Kirstie Rosser. It felt like an oasis in a world dominated by mobile 'phones and microwave meals. A world where increasingly the antidote to a stressful and unhealthy lifestyle is to join the local health club and exercise on a bicycle that goes nowhere.

To experience the sky above and the stream below, the sun on your back and the sounds of running water and reed warblers is such a joyous experience. The knowledge that the harvested rush would provide hours of creative enjoyment throughout the coming year adds to the joy. Being able to follow the whole process through from the planting of a seed to growing it is something we do not do enough of. When you cut the rush yourself you value each one. It is experiences such as this that are few and far between. The pleasure is in its simplicity and the deep satisfaction gained from connecting with the natural environment. Having spent many years working in community education and with an enduring passion for anything creative, my focus in life is to share and encourage others to experience such pleasures.

Working at the Yarner Trust, an educational charity based in North Devon, and living on their organic smallholding, I now organise courses, workshops and residentials in anything sustainable and environmental. The Trust offers courses ranging from straw-bale building to alternative funerals, yurt making to willow basket making and of course the occasional rush workshop. We have recently created a demonstration organic kitchen garden, planted a living willow play environment and organised several successful arts holiday weeks.

The common thread that links our work is the ideal of living in harmony with our surroundings, encouraging others to tread more lightly on the earth. What better way to experience that ideal than rush cutting on the Levels?

John Excell, Rush and Cane

John Excell has been based at his Cane Workshop in Westport for approximately 20 years. He has initiated the move of many individuals (including some of those photographed for this book) towards traditional seat making.

John was trained as a meteorologist, serving his profession for six years in the American Navy. He spent a total of ten years in the States before returning to the UK to set up an antiques business in London. This venture included house clearances where John found a numerous supply of chairs that needed re-seating. This in turn led to evening classes. The business went from selling mostly antiques to restoring seats. The more he undertook the more people wanted the materials and wanted to learn.

In 1978 John and his wife purchased a derelict cottage in Ilminster. As restoration work took place, the more time they spent in Somerset, the more drawn they were to moving away from London permanently. The lease on the shop in London was renewed and sold. John's wife, an audiologist, applied for an East Devon post based in Exeter, one of only six such jobs available in the country.

John's first workshop was a unit on the industrial estate at Ilton. Later on the trustees of the Gospel Hall in Westport heard that John was seeking new premises and approached him with a view to selling. This is where he is based at the time of writing. He sells a full range of seating materials and runs regular workshops at Urchfont Manor College near Devizes.

On 21 July 1999, John became a Freeman of the City of London, a member of the livery of Worshipful Company of Basketmakers, a rare achievement. 'Practical skills,' he says, 'surpass educational qualifications.' 'If you like working with your hands, it's as satisfying as doing anything. At the end of the day it's all about loving what you do. It takes hard work and dedication to produce a quality product that is not simply acceptable.'

A Poem by Sarah Pank, Basket Maker

Absorbing the landscape.

Embracing the elements.

Earth. Rock. Water. Wind.

Walking into woodland.

Welcoming winter.

Weaving willow.

Wandering the hedgerows.

Reclaiming the heart.

Feeling the textures. The sound.

Watching the woods in dormancy.

Awaiting early buds. The awakening.

Receiving the wildness.

Gathering winter's branches.

Larch's colour in clear light.

Collecting hues and stacking bundles.

I weave; to hold, to remember.

For the rhythm, patterns.

For containing. For pleasure. For sharing. To give.

For love.

A Note on Marsh Terms

Bolder: the true bulrush (*Scirpus lacustris*)

Colts: young reed shoots

Feather: the seed head

Flag: the leaf of reed or sedge

Sheaf: mixture of reed with other grasses and fen plants

Single wale: one year's growth/double wale is two years' growth

Butting board: a board for levelling butt ends of reed

Drifter/leggett: a square board on a handle (or aluminium beadle)

Ridge roll: rolls of reed 4ins wide, fastened along the ridge of a roof

Filling in: laying reed along a valley to give a gradual curve

Maigue/meak: a one handed implement with a 2ft curved blade attached to a shortstraight shaft, used by reed cutters.

Staithe: a wharf or landing stage

Note: *There are discrepancies with imperial and metric measurements in this book. This is due in part to the fact that some of the old terms continue to be used today in the workplace.*

Useful Contacts

Amazon Nails (building with straw bales)
Barbara Jones
Hollinroyd Farm
Todmorden
IL4 8RJ

Millichamp & Hall (handcrafted cricket bats)
Rob Chambers
The Willow Yard, Somerset Cricket Ground
Taunton
Somerset
TA1 1YD

Carymoor Environmental Trust
Jill Gilbert (Executive Director)
Dimmer Lane
Castle Cary
Somerset
BA7 7NR
www.carymoor.org.uk
email: enquiries@carymoor.org.uk

Les and Mike Musgrove (willow growers)
Willow Fields, Lakewall
Westonzoyland
Somerset
TA7 0LP
01278 691105
www.musgrovewillows.co.uk

E.M. and H.J. Lock (willow growers)
Lockleaze
Thorney Road
Kingsbury Episcopi
Somerset
TA12 6BQ

D.C. Wright (thatching contractor)
Millway Farm
Compton Dundon
Somerton
TA11 6NX

The Somerset Rural Life Museum
Abbey Farm
Chilkwell Street
Glastonbury
Somerset
BA6 8DB

English Hurdle and Willowbank
Nigel and James Hector
Curload
Stoke St Gregory
Taunton
Somerset
TA3 6JD

The Somerset Willow Company
Aubrey and Darrell Hill
The Wireworks Estate
Bristol Road
Bridgewater
Somerset
TA6 4AP
01278 424003
www.somersetwillow.co.uk